My Walk In a Vineyard With God

Kelly Northway Link

TATE PUBLISHING, LLC

My Walk in a Vineyard with God by Kelly Northway Link

Copyright © 2005 by Kelly Northway Link. All rights reserved.
Published in the United States of America
by Tate Publishing, LLC
127 East Trade Center Terrace
Mustang, OK 73064
(888) 361–9473

Book design copyright © 2005 by Tate Publishing, LLC. All rights reserved.
No part of this publication may be reproduced, stored in a retrieval system or transmitted in any way by any means, electronic, mechanical, photocopy, recording or otherwise without the prior permission of the author except as provided by USA copyright law.

Scripture quotations marked "NKJV" are taken from *The New King James Version* / Thomas Nelson Publishers, Nashville: Thomas Nelson Publishers. Copyright © 1982. Used by permission. All rights reserved.

ISBN: 1-59886-05-8-5

Dedication

Dedicated to the loving memory of

ROBERT "POPPY" LINK

And

JOSHUA M. STRUZYNSKI

Their love, faith and sacrifice
will never be forgotten.

Acknowledgements

A big hug and kiss for my husband, Kevin. Thank you so much for your love, support, encouragement, and "two-cents" during this project.

A very warm hug to Pastor Dave and my church family. Thank you for your love and kindness. Your welcoming arms and love of Christ had helped me to become a new and better person.

Thank you "Me-Me" Link for making me feel like a welcomed addition to the family from day one. And thank you for allowing me to share "Poppy" with others.

My thoughts and prayers continue to go out to Norm, Madonna and Daniel. Thank you for allowing me to share some of Josh's special moments. He was an extraordinary young man, and he touched many lives in his short time with us. He was truly a blessing.

A big thank you to TATE PUBLISHING for helping me share this story with others and fulfilling God's "Assignment."

And to my Lord, who has truly blessed me, and gave me the courage to bring this book to life. Thank you!

Foreword

All of us, whether we admit it or even understand it, are on a spiritual quest. God has imparted to all of us a desire to be reconciled, and to be in union and in fellowship with Him. Unfortunately, most people embark upon this quest in all sorts of various directions that only lead them further away from God, rather than closer. People immerse themselves in their work, in their families, in their play; they seek success and gratification in all the wrong places, and they are left longing for more. Only through Christ can they feel true fulfillment, true joy.

I had the pleasure of sitting under the ministry of a Godly pastor by the name of Ken Craker for sixteen years. He used to speak of the overwhelming joy of being a pastor, and then he would quickly add, also the terrible heartache. As a young man, and a good friend of Ken's, I knew exactly what he meant. Just like certain passages of scripture, we know exactly what they are saying right up until someone else points out more that God has revealed to them.

I was sure that Ken was referring to sharing in the joys and the trials of the people that he was shepherding. Just over five years ago, I became a pastor myself. I quickly learned what Ken meant. God gives some of us glimpses of the future. I'm not trying to be prophetic here, but God allows some of us, (and I believe pastors even more so), to see the lost and to see them stepping into eternity without Him. For those who perhaps are searching for answers, yes, there is a heaven to gain and a hell to avoid at all costs. The heartbreak that Ken referred to was the knowledge that so many people reject Christ and will spend all of eternity in hell.

But I also experienced the joy that Ken referred to as well. The Bible tells us that the angels in heaven rejoice when one that is lost is found. When *one* person accepts Christ, it merits the applause of heaven. The angels are rejoicing; can we do any less? There is truly no greater joy then being in the presence of God when one humbly chooses to accept Christ's forgiveness, and to ask Him into their heart.

Just a little over a year ago, God once again chose to bless me by allowing me to be there for our author, Kelly Link. She was definitely on her own, personal, spiritual quest. At that time, she had read almost the entire Bible cover to cover. She had many questions, some of which she will discuss in her book. She also had a deep longing for the answers that had eluded her for so long. As I attempted to answer those questions, to the best of my ability, I also shared with her the plan of salvation. I asked her if she was interested, and she emphatically answered: "Yes!" What tremendous joy

God allows us to experience here on earth as just a foretaste of what he has waiting for us in heaven!

To borrow a line from her last chapter, that is merely the end of the beginning. Not all of us are going to find our answers in a vineyard, but I can confirm that Jesus is out there waiting for you. Nature itself proclaims His majesty! Perhaps your quest will lead through a vineyard, through the woods, or even down the streets of utter despair. Wherever your quest leads you, I truly hope and pray that it leads you home to Jesus. And I hope that Kelly's journey gives you some guidance and reflection as well. She has completed the first and most essential leg of her journey, how about you?

Pastor David Diffenderfer
Cassadaga Community Baptist Church
Cassadaga, New York

Table of Contents

Acknowledgements.............................. 5
Foreword..................................... 7
Introduction................................. 13

My Testimony 15
  1. My Roots................................ 17
  2. Poppy 25
  3. The Vineyard............................ 35
  4. I Took A "Right" Turn.................... 41
  5. The Search Was On....................... 45
  6. Talent Night............................ 51

My New "Sight" 61
  7. Looking Through God's Eyes.............. 63
  8. The Voice Of An Angel?.................. 65
  9. The Sheep And The Shepherd.............. 69
  10. God's Canvas 75
  11. The Bird And The Bunny 79
  12. Pastor Appreciation.................... 83

The Clay Is Beginning To Take Shape 89
  13. Josh.................................. 91
  14. Watch Night........................... 95
  15. The "Assignment"...................... 99

The End of The Beginning 109
Closing Note................................ 111

Bibliography................................ 113

Introduction

Oh my, where do I start? So much to tell and only so much ink in my printer. I guess the best place to start is at the beginning.

But, maybe before I start my story, I should address one simple question: "Why?"

It took me thirty-four years to find God and Jesus Christ. I have only been a Christian for about a year and so much has changed in my life. I went from an anal-retentive, short-fused individual to a more laid back, easy-going person. Now, I haven't completely gone from one end of the spectrum to the other, but I have noticed the change even a few Christian steps can make.

For example, my priorities have changed. My career used to be my driving force. Now it is God. Before, my thoughts were pre-occupied with job responsibilities: whom to call, what task has to get done first, what time is that meeting, or when do I have to go to New York City for that *other* meeting. Now my thoughts are about my religious journey: the music for the church choir, when is the next church event, what religion-based book should I read next, or it's time to put down my bible so I can take a shower and go to bed.

I am so excited about the changes that have taken place that I wanted to share my journey into Christianity with others. I want nonbelievers to learn the wonders of God and Jesus Christ, and to start asking questions like I did. I want to help strengthen the faith of believers and help encourage them to share their stories. So please continue with me as I share my journey into Christianity.

Now let's start at the beginning . . .

My Testimony

My Roots

My roots are gray. Well, they are really white, but at thirty-five, the specific shade is just a technicality. I have a full head of thick, naturally curly hair, but once I turned thirty, the white hairs started appearing. It's a family trait, but I like to place blame on my husband. I think he is the reason why my hair is changing color so fast.

I used to lighten my hair. That way I could go longer between colorings. Just recently, I decided to go red, which is a natural highlight in my hair, but I noticed I have to color more often. A gentleman from my church noticed my true roots at the part in my hair one Sunday.

"Hey Kelly, what's this?" he said while looking at my head.

"This is hair," I replied. You see, my friend is bald. "I know it has been a while and you may not recognize it, but this is hair."

"No," he replied. "That is not what I'm talking about."

"Oh," I said. "That is a landing strip for the Holy Spirit."

He chuckled and told me that he would accept that for an answer.

I believe God truly loves all His children. Unfortunately, not all His children believe or listen to Him. God has a plan for all of us. Sometimes, He needs to place us in certain situations or certain places, good or bad, in order to get us to listen to Him. I believe this is what God did to me.

I was born and raised in the suburbs of Albany, New York. I attended a local Lutheran church until I was about 10 years old. I don't remember too much about this church. I do remember that I thought the sermons where long and boring. I remember discovering Crayola had a flesh-colored crayon. I remember having a screaming fit during the lighting of my first Advent candle (I had an abnormal fear of fire) and spending the remainder of Advent in the room where my mother once taught second grade Sunday School.

My family started attending a Methodist church until I was in junior high school. I remember being in the youth choir. I once performed with the group and sang a song that allotted for three solo parts. I volunteered to perform one of the solos. Well, they started off as solos, but they turned into duets. I learned about my partner when she called one evening and told me that she was asked by the Director to sing with me so I wouldn't be afraid. Well, I belted out the "solo" so loud that my partner eventually gave up singing. I remember looking to the back of the church and seeing my Kindergarten teacher and wanting her to be able to hear me.

There was a time when my Sunday School class was making wall plaques of the Ten Commandments (my mother still hangs this plaque over her desk). We worked with adult helpers and each person received a sheet of paper with the Ten Commandments. We were to char the edges of the paper and seal it to a charred piece of wood to make it look old. The way this was supposed to work was the adult helper would strike a match and run it along the edge of the paper. The student was to allow the paper to burn for a bit and then gently blow the burning paper out. Easy! Well, with my fear of fire, this task became a little more difficult. My goal was not to char the edges of the paper but to blow the fire out. I became so over zealous in my blowing that not only did my paper receive the minimal amount of charring, but the adult helper had to keep lighting new matches because I would blow out the match along with the paper.

I remember playing "Silent Night" on the piano while the adult choir sang. And I remember walking to the homes of the elderly to sing Christmas carols.

And that's about it. I don't remember what I learned about God and Jesus, other than the more popular stories: the birth, death and resurrection of Jesus, Moses and the Ten Commandments, Jonah and the whale, and Noah and the ark. I do remember learning some songs like "Jesus Loves Me" and "Give God the Glory". I sang these songs while playing on my swing set.

Eventually, it became too much of a hassle for my mother to try to get my family to go to church, so we stopped going. I didn't give church or God much thought after that.

I continued on with life as usual. I graduated from high school in 1987 with special focus in Math, Science and French. I attended the State University of New York (SUNY) College at Brockport, where I received my Bachelors of Science in Biological and Health Sciences. I studied education (kindergarten through twelfth grade) and community education. I had a twelve-week internship with the American Cancer Society, where I taught various health topics at fairs, festivals, and other community organizations in Rochester, New York.

After I graduated, I returned to Albany. I started working through a job placement agency. I was an assistant in a private company. My first permanent job was as a Laboratory Technician, where I conducted HIV screening. Then I worked as a forensic scientist and eventually as a coordinator for a criminal database.

I met a great man and got married in 1997. My husband, Kevin, was in law enforcement, so people naturally assumed that we met at the forensic laboratory. Nope. We met in the lobby of a local animal hospital. I was dropping off my sister's cat to be "fixed" and Kevin was there to pick up his dog. I can remember hearing the door open and watching this man in uniform walk in. He looked like Kurt Russell in the movie "Backdraft." We started talking and learned we had some mutual acquaintances. He talked about his family in Western New York and I talked about my volunteer work with a local rescue squad. Suddenly, my name was called to go in to see the veterinarian. I didn't know what to do. Here I was carrying on a nice conversation with a good-looking man and I didn't know his name! Now I know most people in law enforcement wear a nameplate, which I looked for. But it was December, and he was wearing a coat over his uniform. I didn't know how to ask for this guy's name and phone number (I was too shy to just come out and ask for it.). The veterinarian was waiting to see me (I hate to keep people waiting), so, in a panic, I said "Good-bye" and took my sister's cat into the exam room. In my disgust over how poorly I handled the situation, I started talking to my sister's cat about how I was an idiot.

After I got home, I remembered my ambulance crew chief was good friends with a man my mystery police officer mentioned during our brief conversation. This man was a former military buddy. I called my crew chief, told her the story, and asked her to talk to her friend about getting this guy's name. A week later, my phone rang. When I answered, instead of the usual, "Hello. This is such-in-such," I got "Do you know what I had to go through to find out who you are?" We have been in love ever since.

In January 1997, my grandmother passed away. She left me a small inheritance, which Kevin and I used to buy our first house. We moved about a mile away from my parent's house. In the fall of 1998, my parents announced they bought a house in Tennessee and would soon retire.

My parents' plan was this: put their house up for sale in the spring; my father was going to retire in August and move to Tennessee; my mother would follow shortly thereafter. Well, my parents sold their house in five days! They expected their house to be on the market for a few months, not a few days. They were in a real pickle because they would have their house sold before either one of them was ready to move south. My parents ended up moving in with me and my new husband. At that time, my husband and I owned a raised-ranch and there was a family room, a half-bath and bedroom on the lower floor. This became my parents' temporary home. My husband and I lived on the second floor. The only time my parents came upstairs was to use the shower, the kitchen or to join us in watching television (when we were watching the same programs).

My father retired in August 1999 and moved to his new home in Tennessee. My mother was waiting for a state bill to pass that would give her better retirement benefits. So mom continued to live in the "basement." Mom was in the "basement" almost a year after my father retired. Actually, we sold the house out from under her, but that is the next story.

And so, I was following the American dream, until my life began to change forever.

Poppy

In 1999, my husband's father, Robert (everyone in the family called him "Poppy") was diagnosed with Multiple Myloma. He had a form of cancer that was affecting his white blood cells, and he was given a five-year life expectancy. My husband's family lived in Western New York. We lived in Eastern New York. I know this put a lot of stress on my husband because he was very close to his father.

In the meantime, I was working full time and taking a class towards a Masters in Public Administration. This class was tough because it was so different from classes I took in the past. I was used to science classes and laboratory work. Everything was black and white. Now I was taking a class that was dealing in the gray area, where there was no defined right or wrong answer. I was stressed beyond belief.

On Halloween, I was working on a paper for class when I couldn't take the stress any more. I just threw down my work and went outside to get some air. My husband had been bugging me about raking the leaves in the backyard, so I grabbed the rake and got to work. It was very quiet in my backyard. All I could hear was the rustling of leaves as I raked them in huge piles.

I thought about my life. I was good at my job and it was an important job, but I felt like I had moved up the ladder too fast and there wasn't anywhere left to go. I wanted a Masters degree, but I was in a program that went along with my career and not necessarily what I was interested in. I realized that I needed a change in my career, but what type of job could I get in Albany that wasn't like the job I was currently in? I needed a fresh start.

Then I thought about Kevin's father. It would be nice if Kevin could spend more time with his father during his final years. But could I leave everything I knew and move across the state? I knew this was a big change I was looking at, but could I continue in my current situation? I decided if I didn't take this chance and make a major change in my life now, while I was still young, then it would never happen.

I spoke to my husband about moving to Western New York. He could be closer to his family and I could make a new start. He was excited by the idea. Kevin and I started sending out our resumes. I was surprised how quickly I found a job. I interviewed with a company in Jamestown, New York in November. I was called back for a second interview in February. In the spring of 2000, I was offered a position. Kevin got a job that started a week after mine. Wow! What were the odds of that happening?

I was nervous about telling my mom that Kevin and I were moving. She was still living with us at the time and I didn't want her to be worried about a place to live. She had enough to worry about with my father in Tennessee. This was the longest they had been separated since they were married thirty-six years before.

My mother seemed genuinely excited about my new job. She said she would stay in the house until it sold, then she would get an apartment. It was such a relief to have her living in the house while we were in Western New York. She was there to take care of things until the house sold. As it turned out, Mom finally decided to retire and only had to spend two weeks in a local hotel. I like to think that we finally forced her into retirement.

In April 2000, we loaded up our vehicles with our clothes and our dog (the same dog that Kevin was picking up at the animal hospital where we met) and we left Albany. We moved in with Kevin's parents in Dunkirk, New York. We told them we would only stay there for a month and if we didn't find a house by then, we would move into an apartment. With Poppy's illness, I didn't want him to feel uncomfortable in his own house. But Kevin's parents insisted that we stay as long as needed.

By this time, Poppy had become very weak due to the chemotherapy and the progression of the cancer. Initially, he was "quarantined" to a separate bedroom upstairs that had to be kept very clean. Then Poppy became too weak to go up and down the stairs, so we set up a bed downstairs in a room off of the T.V. room. The whole family remained hopeful that the treatments would destroy the cancer and Poppy would be back to his old self again.

Then on the Friday before Memorial Day, we received some devastating news. The cancer was too far advanced and there was nothing else that could be done. The news hit all of us like a ton of bricks! We went from believing the previous diagnosis that stated Poppy would be with us for at least five years, to the shock of perhaps having him for only a few weeks. We kept asking ourselves, "Why was this happening to such a good man?"

I found myself praying before I went to sleep at night. I asked God to heal Poppy and to return him to the man he once was. I also asked God if this was not meant to be, that He would not let Poppy suffer.

I remember that Memorial Day as the last day Poppy came to the kitchen for breakfast. When he shuffled into the room, I sang a rendition of "Here he comes. Mr. America." For the first time, I noticed how much the cancer had taken a toll on Poppy since he was diagnosed the previous August. Poppy's hair was gone due to the chemotherapy. He had lost a lot of weight. His face was drawn and his color was gray. His movements were slower and the spring was gone from his step. The twinkle in his eyes and his mischievous smile had faded from his face.

Poppy sat at the table, read the newspaper and ate a large breakfast. After that meal, he remained in his room. After a couple days, he stopped watching television and didn't want any visitors.

On Thursday, Hospice came in with a hospital bed and an oxygen machine. That evening, Poppy was having a lot of trouble breathing. My mother-in-law and my brother-in-law, who was a Physician's Assistant, wanted Poppy to go to the hospital. I remember sitting in the chair just outside of Poppy's room watching television. My mother-in-law entered his room and told him of their concern. She asked Poppy if he wanted to go to the hospital. I heard the most forceful "No" I had ever heard from Poppy since he became ill. I smiled and chuckled to myself. He may have been very ill, but he was still strong, still fighting, and still in control.

Friday morning came and I awoke about

5:30 A.M. to get ready for work. I had just finished my shower when I heard my mother-in-law calling me from downstairs.

With my wet hair wrapped in a towel and my body covered in a dark green terry cloth robe, I descended the stairs. My mother-in-law was in the living room. She had been sleeping on the couch since Poppy was moved downstairs. She told me that she could not wake up Poppy. She said he was up around 3 o'clock in the morning. He told her he was having trouble breathing. She said that she didn't want to bother me because I had to work in the morning. She struggled to get Poppy into a more comfortable position, without much success.

Fearing the worst, but remaining calm for the sake of my mother-in-law, I walked into Poppy's room. He laid there between the crisp white sheets, a frail figure of a man—a far cry from the once strong, robust man he was only a few months ago. The only sound in the room was the gentle hissing of the oxygen that came from the breathing tube that rested on the pillow next to Poppy's head. I walked up to Poppy and took hold of his wrist, feeling for a pulse. I placed my other hand on his chest, looking for signs of breathing. Then I placed my head on his chest and confirmed what I already knew. Poppy was gone.

I was not sure how my mother-in-law was going to react to the news, so I decided that I had to remain calm and take charge. I knew I had to keep my mother-in-law busy until the rest of the family arrived. I calmly told my mother-in-law that we needed to call the rest of the family. We went out to the kitchen. My mother-in-law started calling family members while I called my husband and Hospice on my cell phone. It was one of the hardest days of my life. It broke my heart to tell my husband that his father was gone. And all the while, I had to remain strong, composed and in control, in order to keep my mother-in-law together. It wasn't until my husband got home and took over as "The Rock," that I had the opportunity to go upstairs, get dressed and cry. I realized that day that my mother-in-law may appear to be a petite and frail woman, but in reality she was very strong. She did not cry until she was told that Poppy had been taken out of the house.

On the day of the funeral, I woke up feeling a little under the weather. I figured I was tired from the events of that weekend. After the funeral and the luncheon, we returned to the house. I was starting to feel ill, so I went upstairs to lie down. Kevin had invited Poppy's family and friends to the house that evening for one final toast to Poppy.

Kevin woke me just before people started to arrive. By this time, I was into a full-blown flu. The light hurt my eyes, I was nauseous and weak, and my head felt like someone was trapped inside and trying to break out using a sledgehammer. I tried really hard to ignore the illness and go downstairs, but I was too sick. Kevin got me some ginger ale and told me to stay in bed.

I heard people arriving and the murmur of conversations drifting up the stairs. There was only one bathroom in the house, so I was concerned that the bathroom might become occupied when I needed to throw up. I tried to relax. Then, someone managed to lock himself in the bathroom. I started to panic, which did not help my nausea. But the young man was quickly freed from his temporary prison, and I did not have an accident on the floor.

Then I heard Kevin's voice from downstairs. He was asking everyone to quiet down so they could do a toast. I so wanted to be downstairs! I couldn't make out what Kevin was saying, but I lifted my glass of ginger ale and said, "Here's to Poppy!"

Kevin and I remained in Poppy's house until we moved into our new home in August 2000.

The Vineyard

As time passed, my new job in Jamestown was becoming too stressful. I was constantly fighting an uphill battle with employees and supervisors. Things were becoming even more frustrating than when I lived in Albany. This was not the career change I had hoped for. I was desperate to find another job—any other job.

While reading the Sunday Classifieds in the local newspaper, my husband found a listing for a position in a local vineyard. Now, I never knew what a vineyard looked like until I started dating Kevin and he brought me to Western New York to meet his family. But this was usually in the winter when the vines were bare. I didn't know what a grape vine looked like with leaves and grape clusters on it until I moved to Western

New York. How could I possibly be qualified to work in one?

I read the job announcement. I did have the research experience they were looking for as far as conducting experiments, collecting data, and compiling the results for the researchers. I had experience supervising other people. Luckily, the position did not require vineyard experience. The position required a lot of outside work. Up to this point, I worked strictly indoors, either behind a desk or at a laboratory bench. I hardly ever went outside (I wasn't much of a gardener), and my pale Irish skin caused me to burn more frequently than tan. But this job intrigued me. It was so different from any other job I had. It was definitely a complete change from my current career path. My husband encouraged me to apply. What was the worst that could happen?

A week later I received a phone call for an interview. I was amazed. I didn't expect to get this far.

I arrived for the interview and sat down with three people. One was the supervisor, one was an on-site researcher and the other was a future retiree. I was very nervous, but I tried to remain calm, enthusiastic, and professional. I tried to keep things a little light with a few small jokes (more to help me relax). Things started off well until one person asked if I knew anything about grapes. I wanted to crawl under my chair. I only recently learned what they looked like outside of the supermarket. I knew they came in different colors, and some you ate and others were made into wine. That was it. I asked myself, "How do I answer this question without looking like an idiot?" I decided that honesty was the best policy and replied, "I honestly don't know much about grapes other than they grow on a vine." The supervisor smiled and said, "Good. We like honesty. And don't worry; it is not a job requirement. That way, it is easier for us to teach you how *we* want things done." Wow! I impressed them with my stupidity.

After the interview, we walked outside and into the vineyard. Now, picture a young woman in a full business suit and heels walking down the grape rows. I must have been such a sight. The best part was that I never stumbled or tripped. Each step was smooth and confident, like a runway model.

We came across two field workers. They were placing a camera unit into a tube buried in the ground and recording their findings. They must have thought I was nuts and probably too prim and proper to work in a vineyard. I watched the field workers, asked several questions, and then the interview was over and I was on my way home. I felt good. I believed I really could do well at this job and I knew this was the change I needed. I had a feeling the interviewers liked me as well.

The following morning, I learned the vineyard supervisor had called my references right after I left the interview. I thought, "Wow, he must really be interested." The next day, I received a call from my husband. He stated that the vineyard supervisor called and wanted me to call him at his home that evening. I couldn't believe how quickly things were moving. I arrived home that evening and immediately called the supervisor. He once again ran through the job description and benefits. This took about twenty minutes. I paced around the room, waiting for him to get to the good part. When he was done, he asked me if I would be interested, and without hesitating or asking for time to think it over I said, "YES!" My new job started the last week in May 2002.

I had to go out and buy a new wardrobe. Most women would be excited about this. I hate to shop, especially for myself. I did find it funny that I was going from suits to jeans and tee shirts and from high-heels to field boots.

I found that I really enjoyed working in the vineyard. I worked outside everyday unless it was raining or below twenty degrees fahrenheit. I found myself getting a little stir crazy if I worked inside for more than three days. I started working more outside around my house. (I still have a lot to learn about gardening.) I got more exercise walking around the twenty-plus-acre vineyard. I enjoyed the cool shade under the grape canopy. I used lots and lots of sunscreen and still didn't tan.

I witnessed the annual miracle that takes place in the vineyard. I watched the vineyard go from completely bare to beautiful pink flowers in the spring. I watched the green shoots and leaves grow and the development of the grape clusters. I saw the grape clusters change color in the late summer. And I saw the season end as the leaves turned yellow and then dropped off in the fall.

I also learned more about nature. I learned how to identify the sex of a turkey by its droppings. I learned to recognize the difference between a rabbit, a raccoon, a turkey, and a deer by their tracks in the snow. I witnessed a hawk swoop down from the top of a utility pole, fly across the vineyard, and pick up a chipmunk next to a tree. I never thought in a million years that this would be the place for me.

Chapter Four

I Took a "Right" Turn

Since I moved to Western New York, I found people more openly talking about their religious beliefs. And I found this type of conversation was more accepted without a lot of negative feed back. In Albany, I never really heard people talk about religion, and there was more animosity toward people that did. I remember thinking, anyone that discussed religion was just a "Bible Beater".

In Western New York, it appeared to be more the norm to belong to a church and to openly discuss religious beliefs. Religion was a normal topic of conversation at work. I found myself thinking more and more about God and my beliefs, especially when I worked alone in the vineyard.

In December 2003, a co-worker had some terrible news. Her twenty-two-year-old son, Josh, was diagnosed with an inoperable brain tumor. We were all stunned. How could this kind, caring, hardworking young man end up with such a horrible illness? His life had only just begun. He had just started a new job as an agricultural mechanic. He was looking forward to working in the small vineyard he had purchased. He was a volunteer fireman and had completed numerous courses in firefighting and emergency rescue. Josh was named Firefighter of the Year in 2003. And his mom had nothing bad to say about him. How could this happen? Why would God let this happen?

A few days later, while working alone in the vineyard, I found myself asking the ultimate question, "Do I believe in God?" I thought about this question quite a bit. I thought about the churches I attended when I was a young girl in Albany. I thought about what I learned in Sunday School. I thought about the people I knew and our conversations about God. I looked deep down into my heart and soul and I came up with my answer. I realized that I could not say "No."

Once I had my answer, I decided the next step was to learn everything I could about God. I decided the logical first step was to read the Bible. I used to own a child's Bible when I was a little girl. I did try to read it a few times, but never got much farther than Noah's ark and the great flood. I talked to my mother-in-law, a very spiritual woman, and asked her if she had a Bible I could borrow. She gave me one that was written in the 1970s. She said it was written in the language of the time and would be easy for me to follow. It also included an outline of the Bible, descriptions of each book in the Bible, and a suggested reading plan.

I took the Bible home and set to work. My husband worked the midnight shift and usually slept in the evening before going in. I spent my evenings reading. I watched very little television—usually only when I finished a book in the Bible and didn't want to jump into another one, or when my eyelids got too heavy or my mind was wandering too much to focus on what I was reading. I was surprised how many of the stories in the Bible I remembered learning about in Sunday School. But I was more surprised about the neat stories I didn't know, Isaac and Jacob, Joseph and his brothers, Job, and King David.

At first, I was a little afraid to read the Bible. I thought that the Bible was so holy that my fingers would burst into flame when this sinner turned the page. Thankfully, I was very wrong. I thought the Bible was going to read like a school textbook and be dry and boring. Instead, it was filled with fascinating stories of faith, hope, love, and war. Many evenings, I found it very hard to even put the Bible down. I was so excited about everything I was learning, I would give my husband a "book review" when he got up to go to work. I took notes while I read, mainly of people, places and events. I asked my co-workers questions or we discussed something I recently read.

After spending several weeks reading, I decided that I was ready to take the next step. It was time to find a church.

Chapter Five

The Search Was On

After I said "good-bye" to the year 2003 and "hello" to 2004, I decided it was time to find a church. At this point, I wasn't interested in selecting a church based on religious beliefs. I wanted a church where I would feel comfortable, welcomed, and excited about learning more about God. I wanted a clergyman who gave uplifting sermons that left you feeling inspired and motivated. Plus, I was hoping for (but it was not a requirement) a church close to my house so I would not have to travel far when the lake effect snows hit. (Lake effect—for those of you not familiar with the term, is the condition resulting from a cold front from Canada moving across one of the Great Lakes. The front picks up a large amount of moisture, resulting in a LOT of snow.)

I selected four churches; three based on the fact that I knew someone who attended them, and one where I had attended a wedding and a funeral. So for several weeks, I went church-hopping.

The first church was a local Baptist church. My husband worked with a person who was a member (He is now the Associate Pastor). My husband's friend picked me up at my house and drove me to the church. He took me inside and introduced me to the members of the choir (he was also a member). Then he introduced me to the pastor. Pastor Dave Diffenderfer was very friendly and he wanted me to know that if I had any questions to feel free to ask. He loved to talk about God and Jesus.

I sat in the back of the church with a neighbor and soaked in the surroundings, the beautiful paintings of Jesus, the wooden pews and the sense of belonging. When it was time for the sermon, I was surprised the topic selected by the pastor was in a section of the Bible that I had recently read. He talked about Isaac and Rebekah. Rebekah agreed to become Isaac's wife even though she had never met him. She decided to trust in God and to act on faith. She answered God's calling. The pastor asked the congregation if we were ready to answer God's call. I shook my head, yes. That was exactly why I was here. I was answering God's call.

As I was leaving the church, I thanked Pastor Dave for his kindness. He gave me a hug and once again told me if I had any questions to feel free to contact him. I left this church feeling inspired, welcomed, enthusiastic to learn more, and loved. I knew deep down this was the church I wanted to attend, but I wanted to visit the other three on my list, just to be sure.

I spent the next two Sundays visiting the other churches (I was able to attend two services in one Sunday). One church was too modern and so large I didn't think the minister could ever get to know everyone in his congregation. There were no pictures of Jesus, no pews, and no crosses. The next church reminded me of the Lutheran church I attended as a very young girl. The sanctuary was an exact replication of the church in Albany, but on a much smaller scale. The service seemed to move in a similar manner.

But there was so much going on that I had a hard time following.

The final church made me think of something out of "Little House on the Prairie". It was a quaint old church giving me a feeling of history, community, and bonding. The minister's sermon was very interesting and gave me a lot to think about. I went up to him after the service to let him know what I thought about his sermon. The minister politely shook my hand and then turned to another person to talk. I was taken aback. It seemed like he didn't care what I thought one way or the other.

I drove home that Sunday knowing which church I wanted to attend. It seemed as if all of the signs were pointing to the Cassadaga Community Baptist Church—the church where I was asked if I was ready to answer God's calling. "Well, ready or not, God, here I come!"

I started attending the regular Sunday service and the weekly Bible study. I developed new relationships with other church members. I bought my very own study Bible and continued to read every night.

Then late in February 2004, while working in the vineyard, I received a call on my cell phone from my co-worker. It was more bad news concerning her son, Josh. The tumor in his brain had grown and there was not much the doctors could do. I felt completely helpless. I walked through the heavy snow to another co-worker and told her the news. We stood there hugging each other while we cried. She asked God why he needed to take one of our angels.

That evening was Bible study and after the class I told Pastor Dave about what happened earlier that day. He took me into his office and he talked about Jesus Christ. He asked me if I believed in Jesus Christ and if He was in my life. I thought for a moment. I knew who Jesus Christ was and I believed that he was the Son of God, but I really did not know much about him (I had not gotten to the New Testament in my Bible reading). I was afraid if I said "No", that I would come across as a bad person, and if I said "Yes", I would be lying. I really didn't know how to answer Pastor Dave so I told him that I didn't know. He asked me if I wanted to ask Jesus into my life. I nodded my head, yes. He left his office and returned with the Associate Pastor and his wife. Pastor Dave and I said the sinner's prayer, while the Associate Pastor and his wife prayed with us. I asked Jesus Christ into my heart. There were no trumpets sounding His arrival, but He was there. I felt a great warmth surround me, like the arms of a parent hugging a child. The room was filled with love. My life would never be the same. That evening, Wednesday, February 25, 2004, I walked out of that church and into my new life.

Chapter Six

Talent Night

In March 2004, the Cassadaga Community Baptist Church held a talent night. People signed up to share their talents with the congregation. I wanted to share some part of myself with my church. My first thought was to play the piano or the flute. I took piano lessons as a young girl. Eventually, my mother took over as teacher. I remembered practicing an hour every day. I played in several piano recitals as well. I remembered that my younger sister also took piano lessons. She would learn a song and then try to play it as fast as she could without making a mistake. I think it drove mom nuts. I know it drove me crazy.

I became interested in playing the flute when I was in fifth grade. I played in the school band until I was a senior in high school.

I realized it had been several years since I even touched either instrument. I didn't think there was enough time to practice.

My second thought was to write a poem. While I was growing up, I never thought I was very good at writing. It always seemed to be a struggle to put my thoughts on paper. It wasn't until high school that I began to recognize my talent as a writer. I even had a story published in "The Troubadour," my high school annual publication. My writing continued to develop in college. I took some writing courses (that were required), but I think it was my education classes that fine-tuned my talent.

I was studying to become a teacher. One of my courses taught me how to research and develop a teaching program. This entailed selecting an audience, surveying this audience to determine what topics were of interest to them, interviewing people who knew this audience, and writing an entire program so that any person off the street could teach the topic.

Even though I later decided I didn't want to be a teacher, I have used my writing skills to develop and write SOPs (Standard Operating Procedures) for many of the places I worked. I figured with all of this training and experience, I could come up with a nice little poem for my church. Piece of cake!

I spent my evenings jotting down ideas and trying to come up with something. And each evening I ended up looking at a page of topics with no thought of where to go next. Nothing seemed right. Then one day it hit me. It was like someone smacked me upside the back of my head. Duh! The thought was so strong I immediately went to my desk and wrote. Well, it turned into more of a story (It was three pages long). I couldn't believe how quickly and how completely the story flowed from my pen. When I finished writing, I put my pen down and reviewed my work. I was amazed with the finished product. I realized my poem was actually my testimony.

The night of the talent show finally arrived. The evening started with a dinner in the Fellowship Hall. Everyone brought a dish to share. At six o'clock, everyone moved to the sanctuary to begin the show. One of the people seated in front of me had a handwritten order of performers. I saw that I was right in the middle of the program. I also noticed that most of the people performing were either singing or acting out a skit. I was the only one reading a poem.

The show began and I sat in my pew overcome with nerves. I prayed to God to be with me. Then it was my turn. Pastor Dave introduced me by saying, "We are going to have something that has not been done in the past. Kelly is going to read a poem." Well, great—like I wasn't already nervous.

I stood at the pulpit and took a deep breath. Then I began to read my story. I scanned the congregation as I read, looking for their reaction (and hoping I wouldn't lose my place). One of the skills I learned in college was to look at your audience when you spoke. This made the audience feel more involved in what you were saying. I noticed that most every eye was glued on me. There were a few bowed heads and I thought I was putting them to sleep, until I noticed that their heads where nodding in response to my reading. When I finished, I returned to my seat to the sound of applause. I felt great! God had helped me through it.

It wasn't until the talent show was over that I realized the impact my story had on the congregation. Several people came up to me, hugged me, and told me I had them in tears. They loved my story. Little did I know that this was only the beginning.

Later, I learned even Pastor Dave was brought to tears (he was seated behind me during the talent show, so I could not see his reaction). I discovered that Pastor Dave thought his sermon about Isaac and Rebekah was not one of his better sermons. I assured him it was the sign I was looking for when I was searching for a church. It was how I knew I was in the right place.

The following is the story I read on talent night:

A Gentle Knocking
Throughout my life, there had
been a gentle knocking,
Like the knocking on a door.
But I was too busy to listen.
Too busy working,
Too busy going to school,
Too busy rushing about,
Too busy worrying about tomorrow.

I couldn't hear your call.
A change of scenery;
A new home,
A new job,
But the same unchanged heart.
And it was still there,
The gentle knocking.
Something was missing,
But I didn't know what.
I had a place to live,
A loving husband,
My health,
A good job,
Some change in my pocket,
BUT WHAT WAS I MISSING!
Then one day,
Out in the middle of the vineyard,
All became quiet.
Then I heard it,
The gentle knocking.
"Do you believe?"
It was not a loud, thunderous voice,
But a calm, soothing voice.
A voice filled with great wisdom and patience.
"Do you believe?"

Then I realized who was speaking to me,
Who had been with me all along.
I thought for a long moment.
I thought about my life:
What I learned as a child in Sunday School,
And what I learned as I grew older.
And then I realized,
I couldn't say "No".
Then the voice spoke to me once more,
"I have a book, a great book in my word,
that will teach you what I have done."
I started to read this great book,
The Bible.
I found that I could not put this book down.
As I read each verse,
Each chapter,
Each book,
My need to know more grew within me,
As well as my desire to be with other
people who felt the same need.
Then the voice spoke to me again,
"Go to my house where you can learn more."
I visited a few churches,
Looking for a place that felt comfortable.
But I was also looking for something else.

A sign that would let me know
that I was in the right place.
And I heard it.
It was a sermon from Genesis 24.
Abraham wanted to find a wife for his son, Isaac.
It was a sermon about Rebekah.
She had never met Isaac.
Upon faith, she agreed to return
with a servant of Abraham.
She answered the call of God
to become Isaac's wife.
We were asked if any one of us would
be willing to "answer the call".
Yes, Pastor Dave.
I am here to answer God's call.
Some time passed.
I continued to read the bible every day,
As well as attend a weekly prayer group.
Then came the gentle knocking.
"This is my Son. He died for your sins upon
the Cross. Will you ask him into your life?"
Yes, oh yes, My Lord Jesus!
Please come into my life and into my heart!
And in one brief moment,
After one simple prayer,

He was there.
There was no fanfare,
No loud trumpets sounding his arrival,
But a gentle calm.
I was wrapped in a special warmth.
The warmth you only feel when you are hugged
by someone who deeply loves you.
I no longer feel an empty spot in my soul,
Like something is missing.
I have found a peace that has enveloped me.
I am filled with hope and praise,
Faith and joy.
But most of all,
LOVE.
I know that I am loved not just by my husband,
Not just by my family,
Not just by my church family,
But by my Lord and Savior, Jesus Christ.
Thank you, Lord, for continuing
to knock on that door,
Even when I would not listen.
I am listening now.

Kelly Link
March 2004

My New "Sight"

Chapter Seven

Looking Through God's Eyes

"The lamp of the body is the eye. If therefore your eye is good, your whole body will be full of light." (Matthew 6:22 NKJV)

Since I became a Christian, I noticed a change in my lifestyle. I loved to read. After I read the Bible, I wanted to read books that better explained some of the books in the Bible, or biblical people and places. I began to build quite a library of Christian resources. I found myself buying books faster than I could read them.

I didn't watch as much television as I once did. I read more. When I did watch television, I noticed I no longer enjoyed many programs that I once did. I even became embarrassed by many commercials that had very sexual undertones.

During the day, I found myself thinking more about God and Jesus Christ. I even found myself talking to them when I worked alone in the vineyard. Along with this, I found myself looking at things very differently. It was as if God removed a filter from my eyes and allowed me to view the world more clearly. I started to keep a journal of the things I have seen. The following chapters are some of these stories.

Chapter Eight

The Voice of An Angel?

"And He said to me, 'My grace is sufficient for you, for My strength is made perfect in weakness." (2 Corinthians 12:9a NKJV)

  I always wished I could sing. Music was so uplifting and full of emotion. I wanted to be able to express myself through song.
  Several weeks after I started attending the Cassadaga Community Baptist Church, I expressed an interest in joining the choir. I wanted to express my love and appreciation to God by singing praises to Him. I was welcomed into the choir with open arms. But I soon became aware of my lack of a singing voice. I tried as hard as I could. I practiced every evening, but I sounded horrible.

The rest of the choir always sounded so beautiful. There were only seven other choir members, but they always filled the church with angelic voices. I sounded much less than angelic. I was afraid of bringing the quality of the choir down.

I started praying to God, asking to be blessed with a beautiful singing voice. Day after day I prayed, and Sunday after Sunday my voice still sounded like a choking goose. Then I thought I was being too greedy in my request to God, so I started praying for a moderate singing voice. Once again, day after day I prayed, and Sunday after Sunday my voice still sounded like a cow with laryngitis. When I finally realized that God was seemingly not answering my prayer, I became very depressed. I wanted to quit the choir, but the other members would not let me go. They tried to reassure me that my voice was fine. They explained the choir was a blending of voices. I stayed on not because of guilt, but because I enjoyed being in their company. They were becoming a part of my family.

Then I was inspired to write two stories ("A Gentle Knocking" and "I am the Sheep, He is My Shepherd), which I read to the church congregation. After the second story, I decided to keep a journal to write about things God showed me during my spiritual journey.

We hate to admit it, but like any father, God knows what is best for us and sometimes has to say "No" to our requests. It is not that He is being mean, it is just that He has very special plans for us, and sometimes our desires do not fit into His plan. God helped me to realize that while I am not a talented singer, I am a talented writer. God has opened my eyes to the world around me and He has helped me to see things in different ways. By writing down the things He teaches me, I can pass on his word through my pen (or typewriter or computer).

I am still a member of the church choir, but in a new role, as Choir Director. Those that can't sing lead others that can!

Chapter Nine

The Sheep and The Shepherd

"I am the good Shepherd; and I know My sheep, and am known by My own. As the Father knows Me, even so I know the Father; and I lay down My life for the sheep".
(John 10:14–15 NKJV)

When I first read this verse during my Bible reading, it reminded me of a time when I was a young girl attending the Lutheran church in Albany, New York. Four Sunday School students were selected to do a presentation before the church congregation. These students were to be dressed as animals, and to read some prepared lines. There were two boys and two girls selected. I was one of the girls. I don't remember what animals the two boys were dressed as (one may have been a lion), but the two girls were dressed as a peacock and a sheep. I was the sheep. Now I wasn't very excited about being dressed as an ordinary barnyard animal. *What was so exciting about a sheep? Wasn't there some other strong or majestic animal I could be? How about a cheetah, or a swan, or an eagle?*

On the day of the presentation, everyone gathered around the girl dressed as a peacock. They "oohed" and "awed" over her costume. No one was "oohing" and "awing" over the girl in the white jumper and the square cardboard hat covered in cotton balls. Why should they? I was only a sheep. But I stood tall before the large congregation and delivered my lines with confidence and true heart that could be heard clear to the back of the church. I many not have been excited about being a sheep, but I was proud to stand before the church congregation and read God's word. The other "animals" didn't fair as well.

I returned my thoughts to the verse before me. I realized a sheep is not just an ordinary barnyard animal. It is a special member of the flock before the Good Shepherd, Jesus Christ. I realized I am still a sheep and very proud to have the Lord as my Shepherd.

I was suddenly inspired to write the following story, which I read before my church congregation:

I Am the Sheep. He is My Shepherd

When I close my eyes, what do I see?

I see a little sheep that has lost her way. She is wandering the dark forest, trying to find her way back to the green meadows. Her coat is matted and gray. She slowly moves forward, taking each step as if she expects something to reach up and grab her and pull her below the ground. She shivers from the cold, longing for the warmth and safety of the flock. Her eyes dart back and forth; watching for the Wolf that she knows is close by.

The little sheep closes her eyes and pictures the beautiful lush fields she once used to graze. The sweet green grass flowed like a river in the warm breeze. She saw many other sheep in the field, and the Shepherd as he tended the flock. The little sheep wished she did not leave the lush fields, the companionship of the other sheep, and the safety of the Shepherd. But she was tempted by the promise of even sweeter grass on the other side of the hill. Her pride made her believe that she could live without the guidance of the Shepherd. But she only found the lonely, dark forest she was in now.

Then the little sheep hears a strange sound. She stops and listens. Is it the Wolf coming to devour her? No, the sound fills her with warmth rather than despair. Then she realizes that someone is calling her name. The little lost sheep is filled with great hope. Someone is looking for her. Someone wants to save her from this cold, dark place. A light appears at the edge of the woods. It is the most beautiful light the little sheep has ever seen. And standing in the middle of the light is the figure of a man. The man is calling to her. The little sheep takes a few steps and then stops, afraid that this is another trick. Then the man steps forth from the light. The little sheep's face lights up as she recognizes the man standing in the light.

It is the Shepherd.

The little sheep turns from the darkness and runs toward the Shepherd, who stands with outstretched arms. The Shepherd embraces the little sheep. He strokes her coat, turning it white as the new fallen snow. He buries his face into the soft wool, as the little sheep nuzzles her face in His.

Suddenly, the great Wolf jumps out of the darkness. His eyes are a blaze with fire and his teeth are stained red from the blood of his last victim. The Wolf stands before the Shepherd with his fur raised and a snarl on his face. He demands the return of the little sheep. She now belongs to him.

The Shepherd raises his right hand before the Wolf and says, "I am the Good Shepherd. I gave my life for this sheep, so that one day she will be with me and my Father in the most beautiful pasture. You have tried to deceive her and lead her into darkness. But she knows me and believes in me. So I have come searching for her. I have come for my lost sheep. Now go, Wolf, and return to your dark territory. You will not have this sheep. For I am the Good Shepherd."

The Wolf, knowing he has lost this little sheep lets out a great howl. Then he turns and runs back into the dark forest.

The Good Shepherd turns and carries the little sheep back to the beautiful field and the rest of His flock. The Good Shepherd says, "Do not be tempted by promises of better fields and pastures. For I am the Good Shepherd and I will always love and protect my flock. And if you continue to follow me, I will always provide you with beautiful meadows, a warm breeze, and fellow sheep. And one day, I will take you to meet my Father and what a glorious day that will be! But if you wander off again, I will go looking for you. Because I am the Good Shepherd and he who believes in me is always a member of my flock."

Chapter Ten

God's Canvas

"I set My rainbow in the cloud, and it shall be for the sign of the covenant between Me and the earth. It shall be, when I bring a cloud over the earth, that the rainbow shall be seen in the cloud; and I will remember My covenant which is between Me and you and every living creature of flesh; . . ."
(Genesis 29:13–15a NKJV)

One thing I had noticed since I moved to Western New York was the sky. Now I noticed the sky before when I lived in Albany, but the sky in Western New York is much more dramatic. I live southeast of one of the Great Lakes: Lake Erie. I know the weather movement over this large body of water causes very unusual cloud patterns. Oh, we have the usual cloud patterns (cumulus, stratus, cirrus and nimbus), but sometimes the clouds fill the sky and become very puffy and wavy, with different shades of gray mixed in. Many times it makes me think of the sky in some old black and white horror movie. All that is missing is the eerie thunder and lightening.

The sky out here is much more colorful. I saw the Northern Lights for the first time. It was so awesome! The blues and the pinks rolled across the night sky like waves on the ocean.

There is a saying of my maternal grandmother that I find myself repeating "Red sky at night, sailor's delight. Red sky at morn, sailors be warn." (The actual saying is "Red sky at night, sailors delight. Red sky in morning, sailors take warning.") The reason I find myself repeating this saying is because of the vivid red sunsets and sunrises here in Western New York. Many times I find myself looking out the window over my kitchen sink to find that everything has a pink hue to it. It makes me think of a television set needing the color adjusted because everything looks green. This is how the evenings and mornings can look, only in shades of pink. It almost feels like time has stopped and you are in a different plane of being.

The sky is also filled with the most vividly colored rainbows I have ever seen. I was working in a vineyard with four other people when I looked up and just in front of me was the most perfect rainbow. I stood in awe at its beauty. Everyone else stopped working to gaze upon God's gift. I turned to the person closest to me and I asked him if he knew what the rainbow stood for. He knew I meant something other than the refraction of light through water, so he remained quiet waiting for my answer. I told him that it was a sign, a reminder of God's promise to Noah and to all of us that He would not flood the earth again. Then a second or double rainbow appeared above the first. This is a rainbow where the colors are in reverse order: from violet to red instead of red to violet. My co-worker asked me what the second rainbow stood for. I told him that this was God's explanation point!

Chapter Eleven

The Bird and The Bunny

"God is love, and he who abides in love abides in God, and God in him. Love has been perfected among us in this: that we may have boldness in the day of judgment; because as He is, so are we in this world. There is no fear in love; but perfect love casts out fear, because fear involves torment. But he who fears has not been made perfect in love. We love Him because He first loved us." (1 John 4:16b-19 NKJV)

    In August 2004, I had two very different experiences, but both together meant something big.

    Earlier one week, I went up into the attic at work. I can't remember what drew me up the stairs. Once up there, I discovered a little bird trying to get out. It would fly from one end of the attic to the other, trying to get out one of the closed windows. I followed the bird, back and forth, talking to it, trying to calm it down so I could catch it and take it outside. The little bird just kept flying away from me and banging its head against the closed windows. I was able to get one of the windows opened, so I kept trying to direct the bird out the open window. But instead, it would go to the window next to it or the window above, but not out the open window. A few times, it got caught between the panes of glass and I had to get it out. It fought me all the way, and flew from my hands once it was free. I began to get frustrated with this stupid bird. Didn't it understand that I was trying to help it?

Then I thought about when I was like the little bird, flying away from God when He was only there to help me. I did not listen to or trust God enough to accept his helping hand and words of wisdom. Instead, I kept flying into closed windows because I was closed to God.

A few days later, while working at my desk, a co-worker came in from cutting the tall grass in the fields. In his hands was a tiny wet bunny. He placed the bunny in my hands and left. I was surprised the little bunny wasn't shaking and it wasn't struggling to get free. I talked softly to it, reassuring the little bunny that it was safe. I placed the bunny on my chest and gently stroked his wet fur, as I continued to talk to it. Then the most unbelievable thing happened. The little baby bunny went to sleep. I was amazed. This little "wild" creature felt comfortable and safe enough in my arms to go to sleep. I was filled with such awe, warmth, and excitement. I almost can't describe the joy I was experiencing!

Then I thought about God. *Was this how He felt when we accepted Him and worshiped Him, and allowed ourselves to feel comfortable and safe in His embrace?*

I realized I have changed a lot over the last several months. I went from the scared little bird, which kept flying away from God's call, to the little baby bunny filled with comfort and safety in His presence. I can only imagine the joy God feels when one of his special creatures completely turns toward Him.

"Thank you, Lord, for allowing me to have this very special experience. And thank you for your comforting embrace. I love you, dear Heavenly Father. Amen."

Chapter Twelve

Pastor Appreciation

"And we urge you, brethren, to recognize those who labor among you, and are over you in the Lord and admonish you, and to esteem them very highly in love for their work's sake."
(1 Thessalonians 5:12–13a NKJV)

In October 2004, my church held a "Pastor Appreciation" day. This allowed members of the church congregation to show their appreciation for the work Pastor Dave has done. I have never participated in this event, so I asked the Associate Pastor what takes place on this day. He stated that there is special music, a skit, and the Associate Pastor gives the sermon. He stated that anyone who was interested could do something to show his or her appreciation. In the back of my head, I was thinking of writing one of my stories to include in a card especially for Pastor Dave. I mentioned to the Associate Pastor that I was thinking of doing this, but I left out the part about the card and just mentioned writing a story.

I found myself having trouble coming up with a story for Pastor Dave's card. Everyday, I sat down and jotted down ideas, but nothing materialized. I even got up early the morning of that special Sunday, but still couldn't come up with anything. I decided that I would try to write something after the morning's service and give Pastor Dave his card at the service scheduled for that evening.

Since the choir was not singing, I sat in a pew toward the front of the sanctuary. I started looking over the service program and saw my name listed as one of the presenters. I went into a panic! I didn't have anything prepared. I jumped up and went to the Pastor's office. I told the Associate Pastor that there was a misunderstanding. I did not plan on writing a story to present to the congregation, but to include in a personal card. He said not to worry; I didn't have to do anything if I was not ready. I sighed with relief and returned to my pew.

But instead of feeling relaxed, I felt guilty. I felt like I did something wrong by telling the Associate Pastor that I would not give a presentation. There suddenly was a very strong desire in my heart to just do the presentation; that the words would be there. I felt a very strong push from God to trust Him. I saw the Associate Pastor's wife and called her over. I asked her to go tell her husband that I changed my mind and that I would do the presentation.

The service began and the music and sermon were beautiful. I kept praying to God to give me the words for Pastor Dave. Then it came to my part in the service. The Associate Pastor turned to me and asked me if I still wanted to come forward. I nodded, yes. He introduced me and I walked to the front of the church and stood at the pulpit. I had a small card with me that had a picture of Jesus Christ. I looked at this picture, said one final prayer, and then I began.

I started by explaining to the congregation that I didn't have anything prepared. I told them about the misunderstanding between me and the Associate Pastor, but that I suddenly had a very strong desire to come before them and tell my story. I told them that this story was coming from my heart.

I told the congregation I was a sheep and I was very proud to be a sheep. I told them that at one time, I was not so happy about being a sheep. I told them about the presentation I gave as a small child where I was dressed as a sheep (see Chapter Nine "The Sheep And The Shepherd").

Next, I explained that all of us are sheep in a flock. Then I informed the congregation that I was going to use the term "herd", even though it may be incorrect. I explained I was nervous and didn't want to slip and say a word incorrectly.

I told the congregation I had thought about sheep herds and their shepherds. I believed if the herd was large, there would be one Shepherd who was responsible for the entire herd, and several other shepherds that would be responsible for watching over and protecting smaller groups of the large herd. I reminded the congregation that Jesus Christ is the "Good Shepherd" and the Shepherd that watched over the entire herd. This made Pastor Dave responsible for watching over our small herd under the guidance of the "Good Shepherd".

Jesus cares for His sheep. He keeps them close and safe. God goes after those that have wandered off. He heals their wounds. He guides and protects them. Most of all, He loves them.

I stated that Pastor Dave follows in the same suit as the "Good Shepherd." He cares for every one of us here. He is there when we are sick or sad or hurt or happy. He shares in our sorrow and our joy. He is enthusiastic about the Lord and wants to share Him with everyone. He is always there with a kind word and a warm hug. He goes after those who have drifted away from Christ and helps to guide them back to Him. Most of all, he loves each and every one of us.

I turned toward Pastor Dave, who was sitting in the congregation. I thanked him for everything he had done for us and that we all care for him deeply. I told him we are all very proud to be members of his flock. (And I was glad I said the correct word!)

"Thank you dear heavenly Father for using me as your vessel to express the wisdom of your word, to show appreciation for our Pastor, and the love of your son, Jesus Christ. Amen."

The Clay is Beginning to Take Shape

Chapter Thirteen

Josh

In Chapter Four, I mentioned a young man named Josh, the son of a co-worker. He was diagnosed with brain cancer. His illness led me to question my religious beliefs. He helped direct me down the path to God and Jesus Christ. But there was more to his story.

In Western New York State, there is an organization called "Former Troopers Helping Hands." It is a non-profit organization made up of retired New York State Troopers (State Police). They raise money to assist children and families with special needs. They try to make special dreams come true. This organization approached Josh about his special wish.

Josh's wish was to visit Washington D.C., but the tumor had made him too weak to walk and part of his body was paralyzed. Josh was asked if there was anyone special he would like to meet. Josh named some famous political and religious figures. He did say he would like to meet the President and First Lady, but the President was in the middle of his campaign trail for re-election. (The President and First Lady did send a very nice picture and letter to Josh.)

Josh then decided he wanted one last celebration with his family and friends. In the summer of 2004, the "Former Troopers Helping Hands" organized a barbeque. Josh had a large family, and all firefighters become brothers, so there was some concern over the space available for the barbeque. It was decided that family and fellow firefighters would be invited to the actual barbeque. An hour to an hour and half would be set aside so everyone had a chance to enjoy the food. Then the hall would be opened to additional friends. Following the barbeque, everyone was able to enjoy a local country band that donated their time to be with Josh and his friends and family.

Up to this point, I had never met Josh in person. I've seen pictures of him, and I saw him at a fundraiser held earlier in the year by the Fire Department in which Josh was a member. But we were never formerly introduced.

My husband and I arrived at the local Fire Hall to see what appeared to be hundreds of people in attendance. I looked for Josh and his family. I spotted him near the stage. I was shocked at how much he had changed. Josh had grown too weak to walk, so he was in a wheelchair. He had put on weight due to the steroids he was taking to control the ill effects of the tumor. He was having difficulty with double vision, so he was wearing an eye patch. The cancer was beginning to take its toll on this brave young man.

I approached the family and gave my co-worker a big hug. She introduced me to her son. I bent forward and took Josh's hand. I smiled warmly and said "Hi." I looked straight into his eye and was amazed with what I saw.

For a brief moment, everything around me seemed to stop. I was drawn into a light that seemed to emanate from Josh's bright blue eye. I did not see sadness, anger, grief or despair. Instead, I saw strength, courage, faith and hope in this young man. I was in a trance. I did not want to move for fear of losing this special moment. I felt as if I was peering into a window directly to God. I wanted to wrap this young man in my arms so that I could feel this power of the Holy Spirit. And as quickly as the moment began, it was over. Josh was introduced to another attendee, and my husband and I stepped aside.

I will never forget the special moment Josh shared with me. His courageous battle and never ending faith helped me to re-evaluate my life and strengthened my faith. Unfortunately, I never had the opportunity to tell Josh how much he had helped me on my journey to Jesus Christ. Josh's soul and spirit left us on November 13, 2004. He was twenty-three years old.

"Thank you dear Lord for sharing this wonderful young man with so many people. While his time on earth was short, he touched many, many lives, including mine. I will never forget his blessing or his sacrifice. Please continue to be with his family during their time of grief. For you know what they are experiencing, since you also sacrificed your son, Jesus Christ. Amen."
Thank You Josh!

Chapter Fourteen

Watch Night

The "Watch Night" service at the Cassadaga Community Baptist Church was a special time to gather together in fellowship, reflect on the blessings of the past year, and pray for continued blessings for the New Year. December 31, 2004 was my first "Watch Night" service. I arrived at the church around 7:00 P.M. Several members of the congregation were already there and were busy taking down all of the Christmas decorations. They did it so fast, I wished they would come to my house and help me. When we finished, we gathered in the Fellowship Hall. Everyone had brought a dish to share. We ate and played games.

The first game was a guessing game. One selected church member had index cards with various names on each one. She pinned a card to each person's back. That person had to guess the name on their card by asking other people "yes" and "no" questions. Some people guessed the name right away. Some of us took a little longer.

After everyone guessed the name on their card, people began to gather into different groups. Some of the groups played games, while others just talked and enjoyed the fun-loving atmosphere.

At eleven o'clock, we gathered in the sanctuary for the service. Pastor Dave began by requesting any testimonies from the congregation. I raised my hand. When I was selected, I told everyone about a recent conversation I had with my husband.

The conversation took place in the church parking lot following the Christmas Eve Service. When my husband and I got into our car, he leaned over to me and gave me a big hug and kiss. He told me he was so proud of me (I had performed a skit for the service). He commented on how much I had changed since we moved here from Albany. I sat back for a moment and thought about what he had just said. I realized that he was right. I did change a lot. And most of that change had happened over this past year!

Just over a year ago, I heard God in a vineyard. He directed me to this church. He taught me about His Son, Jesus Christ, whom I asked into my heart. I became a member of the church choir and then the Choir Director. I had filled in for the church pianist when she was away visiting her family. I was asked to direct the Sunday School youth band for the annual Children's Day Sunday Service. I had written stories, which I had presented to the church congregation. WOW! When I lived in Albany, I would never have thought I would be doing anything like this. But God knew I would. He knew all along. It was His plan for me.

Then I thought about all of the things I had learned while growing up that I had used over this past year. I realized God had been working in my life long before I turned toward Him. As a young girl, God taught me how to play the piano. I used this skill as the back-up church pianist. When I got a little older, God placed me in the school band and chorus where I watched the movements of the Directors. I used what I learned to lead the church choir and the Sunday School band as Director. When I was in High School, God taught me how to write stories. I had written stories for the church publication and for special church services. In college, God taught me how to talk in front of large groups of people. I have read and performed many of my stories to the church congregation. All along He had prepared me for this special time in my life when I would use the skills He had given me to further spread His word.

I was floored. It was like all of the pieces of the puzzle had fallen into place. Everything seemed to make sense. There was a deeper purpose to my life. It was to be a vessel for God to further spread His word, and to touch His children in a new and exciting way. I was so excited to be on this new journey with God. I couldn't wait to discover what God had in store for me in the following year.

Chapter Fifteen

The "Assignment"

"For I know the thoughts that I think toward you, says the Lord, thoughts of peace and not of evil, to give you a future and a hope. Then you will call upon Me and go and pray to Me, and I will listen to you. And you will seek Me and find Me, when you search for Me with all your heart." (Jeremiah 29:11–13 NKJV)

Sunday, November 27, 2004 started out as a normal day. I got up, went to church and sat in a pew toward the front with my husband, Kevin. Little did I know this sermon would send me on a whole new journey with God.

This particular Sunday, Pastor Dave started the sermon by discussing a project called "The Kingdom Assignment" (Bellesi, 2001).

Before he went into any further details, Pastor Dave asked for ten volunteers to take on this "Assignment." He said this project would require a lot of faith, a lot of hard work, and a lot of prayer. I had recently felt like I was lacking in my spiritual devotion to God, and this project sounded like it was the boost I needed to get back on track. I quickly volunteered and stood in front of the church congregation. Several other volunteers quickly joined me. Then Pastor Dave presented each one of us with a crisp, new one hundred dollar bill. Then he explained "The Kingdom Assignment."

This project comes from the book *The Kingdom Assignment* by Denny and Leesa Bellesi. They spent many years developing their ideas before first presenting this "Assignment" to their church congregation in Southern California. The basis for the "Assignment" was that the Kingdom of God was not just in heaven, but also in each one of us who had asked Jesus Christ into our life. This was also stated in Luke 17:20–21:

"Now when He was asked by the Pharisees when the kingdom of God would come, He

answered them and said, "The kingdom of God does not come with observation; nor will they say,' See here!' Or, 'See there!' For, indeed, the kingdom of God is within you." (NKJV)

In order for this kingdom to grow, we must tap into the blessings given to us by God.

Pastor Dave then explained there were only three requirements to this "Assignment." First, the money given to each of us was God's money. It did not belong to us or to the church. Second, we had to invest this money in a way that would extend God's kingdom. Third, in ninety days, we were to share with the church congregation what we did with God's money. And that was basically it. For a moment, I was gripped by fear. What had I gotten myself into? What was I going to do? When was I going to have time to do it?

Before I became too entangled in fear's grip, I thought about the wonderful things God had done for me over the short period of time I had followed Him. I knew with my faith in God and His son, He would guide and direct me through this project. Then I was struck by an idea.

I could write a book.

Since I started sharing my stories with the congregation, many people have suggested that I write a book. I always smiled and told them that it was something to think about. Writing a book seemed like a full-time project. I couldn't find time to complete regular, everyday tasks, let alone take on a project of this magnitude. So I never gave it any serious thought.

This "Assignment" brought the idea of writing a book from the back burner to the front. But the fire wasn't too hot. Christmas was right around the corner and there was a lot to do.

Early in December, I came down with a terrible cold that had me laid up for a week. I was getting a late start and decided I didn't need any added stress, so I didn't give the book much thought.

Once the New Year arrived, I decided it was time to stoke up the fire and get serious about this "Assignment". In my mind I thought the book could be a composite of the stories I had presented to the church congregation, and stories from my personal journal about the new "sight" God had given me. But when I sat down to write the book, I found I had a very difficult time getting started. I didn't know what to write about, how to put it together, or what the main focus should be. I kept changing my mind and jumping from one idea to another: should I write a book, or should I write a children's book, or should I just try to publish some of my stories in a magazine? My head was full of confusion and self-doubt, while the paper remained blank before me. My confidence and enthusiasm for this project quickly began to fade. Did I really think I was good enough to write a book? I started to get frustrated with myself, which made me feel depressed and inadequate, which further hindered any attempts to start the book. I began to feel that I was letting God down.

One day, I was discussing my difficulties with a fellow church member. She reminded me that Satan knew our weaknesses and used them to distract us from God. Bang, she hit the nail right on the head! That was exactly what was happening to me. Satan was filling me with all of these negative thoughts and feelings of self-doubt, which put me in a whirlwind of confusion. Then I took a mental step back. Satan was working very hard (maybe even putting in some overtime) on my insecurities to keep me distracted from writing the book. I thought if Satan was spending so much time and effort to keep me distracted, than this project must be really important to God. Once I came to this realization, the fog immediately cleared. My confidence was strengthened, all negative thoughts began to disappear, and a path was laid out before me. I started moving forward.

The first thing I did was to buy a book on how to write a book. I never attempted anything of this magnitude before and I needed some background information. Then I began jotting down ideas and developed an outline. I sat down at my computer and began to type. I wasn't concerned about exactly what I wrote just as long as the idea was there. I would go back and make sense of it later. I set a goal of three pages a day. I figured this was an easy goal to meet and this would be further encouragement. Of course, if I typed more than three pages a day, then I would be ahead of the game.

In five days, I had the first draft of the first six chapters. In seven days, I had the first draft of the next six chapters. I was completely amazed at how quickly everything came together. While it did help that some of the book's content came from the stories I wrote for church and from my journal, a lot of the book came to me while I sat at my computer or at my kitchen table with pen and paper. When I finally sat back and took a good look at what I had accomplished in a short period of time, I knew that God was working through me. I thanked Him each night before turning off the light.

With the book well on its way, the next step was to figure out how to get it published. I spent my free time during the day (what little I had) researching publishing agencies. I quickly realized that writing the book was the easy part. Getting it published was going to be a whole different ballgame. I knew I wanted an agency that primarily published Christian books. I thought that this was the best avenue since they would have the best appreciation for the book. I soon learned that there are different types of publishing agencies; it was going to be difficult since I was a new author. So I focused on Christian publishers who were interested in first-time authors.

I found some agencies that looked interesting and requested additional information.

Then Satan began working on my insecurities again. I began to worry that I would have the book written, but it wouldn't be good enough to be published. If no one published it, then what would I do? Then one day I received a phone call from one of the agencies I was interested in. The representative called to provide me with any additional information about their agency, and how to submit a manuscript. Now I was just expecting to receive information in the mail. Then I would call them for further information. The last thing I expected was for *them to call me.* It was a sign from God that I was on the right path and to continue to let Him lead me.

When I was finally ready to submit a manuscript, I only sent it to one agency. The thought of having a back-up plan was floating around in my head, but my heart said not to worry. This was where God had led me. He would see it through.

That was the whole point to this "Assignment". We were to reach deep down within ourselves and tap into our God-given talent. Then we were to open ourselves up to God and allow Him to direct us. We were to allow Him to use us as His vessels and witness the wonderful things that would follow. And this book was the end result.

On Sunday, February 27, 2004, I stood before my church congregation and told them about my "Assignment". I described my struggles and frustrations, as well as my progress. Then I had to pause for a moment as I found tears beginning to swell in my eyes and my breath beginning to quiver. I told the congregation that five days earlier, the agency I sent my manuscript to had called and said they were interested in my book. I was so filled with emotion that I wanted to cry. I believe that I didn't truly realize what I had accomplished in less than sixty days until that moment. And it was all because of love and faith in the one true God.

The End of the Beginning

Closing Note

This book had really surprised me, while at the same time; it had further strengthened my faith. In less than sixty days, I wrote a book, sent the manuscript to *one* publishing agency and had it accepted. How else could this have happened so quickly but through the blessings of God. And anytime along the way I had felt any doubt, He was there with a sign of encouragement.

I took a leap of faith and stepped out of my comfort zone. I entered into unknown territory, but I was not alone. God was there guiding me every step of the way. I learned first hand that if you opened yourself up to God and allowed Him to direct you down the path that He had prepared for you, wonderful things would happen.

I truly believe God has a purpose for this book. If my story reaches just one person and brings him or her to Christ, then it was well worth the effort. I hope this book will help everyone who reads it. For the Christian, I hope it further strengthens your belief and encourages you to open yourself up to God and see where He leads you. For those that don't really know where they stand regarding religion, I hope this book encourages you to start asking questions and seeking answers. And for those who don't believe, I hope this book gives you something to think about. Maybe you can start the journey as I did, by taking a walk in a vineyard. God is waiting for you.

I don't think the Lord is finished with me yet. I believe His plan for me continues as the path stretches out before me. I wonder where it will take me. Another book? A new career?

As I step forward, I glance at the road already traveled. It is only a short distance from the starting point, but a lot of changes have taken place. As I move forward, I realize that the beginning of my journey is over. But there is much more to come!

Bibliography

Bellesi, D., L., (2001), *The Kingdom Assignment.* Zondervan, Grand Rapids, Michigan

Order more copies of this book at

TATE PUBLISHING, LLC

127 East Trade Center Terrace
Mustang, OK 73064

(888)361 - 9473

Tate Publishing, LLC

www.tatepublishing.com